Oregano

Oregano

Rose Napoli

Oregano
first published 2018 by Scirocco Drama
An imprint of J. Gordon Shillingford Publishing Inc.

Scirocco Drama Editor: Glenda MacFarlane
Cover design by Terry Gallagher/Doowah Design
Author photo by Ian Brown

Printed and bound in Canada on 100% post-consumer recycled paper.
We acknowledge the financial support of the Manitoba Arts Council and
The Canada Council for the Arts for our publishing program.

Production inquiries should be addressed to:
Talent House
204A St George St.
Toronto, ON M5R 2N5
416.960.9686

Library and Archives Canada Cataloguing in Publication

Napoli, Rose, author
Oregano / Rose Napoli. -- First edition.

A play.
ISBN 978-1-927922-40-8 (softcover)

I. Title.

PS8627.A66O74 2018 C812'.6 C2018-900236-0

J. Gordon Shillingford Publishing
P.O. Box 86, RPO Corydon Avenue, Winnipeg, MB Canada R3M 3S3

For Mimmo

Rose Napoli

Rose is an actress and playwright based in Toronto. Named as an "Artist to Watch" by the *Toronto Star*, *The Globe and Mail*, and *NOW Magazine*, Rose has been nominated for a Dora Mavor Moore Award and a Prix Rideau. Most recently, her play *Lo (or Dear Mr. Wells)* premiered at the Streetcar Crowsnest in 2017 as part of The Consent Event co-produced by Nightwood Theatre and Crow's Theatre. She has been a member of playwrights units with Nightwood, the Thousand Islands Playhouse, and the Tarragon Theatre. Her plays include: *Shrew (A Big Fat Italian Comedy Inspired by William Shakespeare)*, *Ten Creative Ways to Dispose of your Cremains*, and *A Death and the Marias*. *Oregano* is her first play and was shortlisted for the RBC Emerging Playwright Award at Tarragon Theatre. As an actress, Rose has worked around the country and in the US with various theatre companies and in film and television. She was born in Montreal and graduated from the University of Windsor, where she also spent a few years working as a teacher with the Windsor Essex County District School Board.

Acknowledgements

Oregano was presented with support from the Toronto Arts Council and the Canada Council for the Arts. Special thanks to Elana Post, Pierre Brault, Lynne Griffin, Tal Gottfried, Maria Vacratsis, Juan Chioran, Peter Pasyk, Marcia Johnson, and Paula Wing for their assistance in the play's development.

Production History

Oregano premiered at the Storefront Theatre
in Toronto, March, 2015.

Directed by Matthew Thomas Walker

MONA .... Rose Napoli
MIMMO ....Richard Greenblatt
LA SIGNORA STREGA ....Diane D'Aquila

Live Music & Soundscape
Composed and Performed by Beau Dixon

Set and Costume Design: Jenna McCutchen

Lighting Design: Pat Lavender

Producer: Sarah English

Stage Manager: Bryn MacLeod

Study the past if you would define the future.
— Confucius

I would have told him, Once upon a time, you were a fish.
A fish? he'd have asked.
That's what I'm telling you, a fish.
How do you know?
Because I was also a fish.
—Nicole Krauss, *The History of Love*

Your monument shall be my gentle verse
Which eyes not yet created shall o'er-read,
And tongues to be your being shall rehearse
When all the breathers of this world are dead;
You still shall live, such virtue hath my pen
Where breath most breathes, even in the mouths of men.
—William Shakespeare

Characters

MONA...........Twenties, recent graduate, would-be writer

MIMMO......................................Her father, a man, magical

LA SIGNORA STREGA..............A witch, a woman, magical

The Boy (Mimmo Con La Voce) should be played by the actor playing Mimmo. However, it is also acceptable to use a child to represent the boy throughout the play.

Playwright's Notes

The play moves very quickly.
There should be no break between scenes.

It's best if images are not represented literally.

Mimmo's musical theme should be represented in various musical forms.

None of the characters speak with an accent.

Blackness. A wind blowing. A storm is coming.

In the darkness, we hear the voice of a small child singing MIMMO's Theme. Lights slowly rise up and we see THE BOY, eight years old, barefooted, holding a blue umbrella. He sings beautifully. THE BOY runs off as MIMMO, a man of fifty, bursts in carrying a bag of groceries. MONA, his daughter, is the heap on the sofa.

MIMMO: Mona! Mona mia! Wake up!

MONA: Dad?

MIMMO: It's time, my little chipmunk!

MONA: What are you doing? Where were you?

MIMMO: I just ran to the store to pick up a few things.

MONA: What time is it?

MIMMO: Two. Or something like that.

MONA: In the morning?

MIMMO: You promised. Whenever the mood strikes me, I said, and you said fine.

MONA: I didn't realize the mood would strike at two in the morning.

MIMMO: Mona. You promised.

MONA: I have a migraine.

MIMMO: Oh no, you're not doing that.

MONA: It's a bad one, too.

MIMMO: You're not avoiding this.

MONA: Eight out of ten bad.

MIMMO: No no no.

MONA: Verging on 8.5.

MIMMO: Avoiding.

MONA: You're aggravating it now – 9.

MIMMO: Come on, Mona Mona.

MONA: Can't we just do this in the morning?

MIMMO: Tomorrow's Friday. Some of us work, you know. We can't all enjoy post-graduation life breaks.

MONA: Tomorrow's Friday? And I am not post-graduate-ly breaking; I'm post graduate-ly writing.

MIMMO: Seems to me that you're post graduate-ly watching reality television in between naps.

MONA: How about after you're done work tomorrow?

MIMMO: Now. It has to be now.

MONA: I'm not lying about the migraine.

MIMMO: How bad is it actually?

MONA: Seven – but it's moving quickly.

MIMMO: When did it start?

MONA: A few hours ago.

MIMMO: You were doing so good.

MONA: I haven't been taking any of the medication. I didn't even renew the prescription and now a hurricane of the temples. My blood vessels are holding my brain hostage or something.

MIMMO: When was the last time you had one?

MONA: Months! Maybe even a year.

MIMMO: Hm.

MONA: What?

MIMMO: Here we are.

MONA: In our living room?

MIMMO: I had a feeling today. I knew it. I know what's going on here.

MONA: A subarachnoid hemorrhage?

MIMMO: There can be only one logical explanation.

MONA: You are the authority on logic.

MIMMO: La Signora Strega is coming for you.

MONA: What?

MIMMO: She comes to us when we need her the most.

MONA: In the form of an aneurysm?

MIMMO: She's a witch.

MONA: You've been strange all day – what is going on with you?

MIMMO: La Signora Strega. She comes in a shape rounder than a bulbous nose. With a hump on her right shoulder and a wooden spoon for a hand.

MONA: Rounder than a bulbous nose? You're such a thief.

MIMMO: What thief?

MONA: Queen Maab?

MIMMO: I don't know what you're talking about.

MONA: Plagiarism is a serious offence.

MIMMO: La Signora is my story.

MONA: *Romeo and Juliet* is your favourite.

MIMMO: You're the only one that quotes Shakespeare in this house.

MONA: "It is a wise father that knows his own child" – 10, 9…

MIMMO: Oh! I know this one! You read it last month, right?

MONA: 8, 7, 6…

MIMMO: The old man? Ah – what's the one? The sad one!

MONA: 5, 4, 3…

MIMMO: *Lear!* The king! One of the kings! Henry!

MONA: *The Merchant of Venice.*

MIMMO: I knew it was one of the tragedies.

MONA: It's a racist comedy.

MIMMO: I'm getting closer! I'm gonna get one right one of these days.

MONA: You're getting further away.

MIMMO: You're throwing me off-topic with your games, Mona! La Signora Strega! She lives in a slanted house on the edge of a cliff.

MONA: Waiting for the tide to take her away?

MIMMO: Nestled in her chariot, a ripe purple fig, she comes: La Signora!

MONA: Her timing is impeccable.

MIMMO: With her team of garlic cloves and oregano leaves, she comes to young ladies as they sleep and struggle with their dreams.

MONA: Struggle?

MIMMO: That very Strega who carries with her the smell of sizzling pork fat, who leaves trails of meat crumbles wherever she goes. The temples are telling you: She's coming. You can't escape her.

This is She.

MONA: Who plagues the young ladies with pounding temples?

MIMMO: Only the self-torturing ones. And only in the moment of greatest need. She galumphs and tramples through young dreamers' brains and then they dream of –

MONA: Love?

MIMMO: No no, not that. They dream of the past.

MONA: That sounds like a nightmare, Dad.

MIMMO: The past is a useful tool in facing the future. Remember that.

MONA: Were you Googling again?

MIMMO: Pearls of wisdom.

MONA: We do not have unlimited internet, Dad, you're the one who picked the package.

MIMMO: She's coming.

MONA: A witch will galumph (not a word) and trample through young dreamers' brains and then they dream of the past. Which is a useful tool in facing the future.

MIMMO: Exactly.

MONA: An evil witch to save the day? This is your pearl of wisdom?

MIMMO: Nonononono, not evil! Necessary. And once she comes, she never leaves.

MONA: Is this supposed to help with the migraine? Your stories are the least comforting – they're actually stress-inducing.

MIMMO: And yet, you are my most dedicated audience. Oh, Mona Mona! It means something is about to happen. Something big.

MONA: My intracranials are bursting.

MIMMO: Can you ever just relax?

MONA: You're the worst.

MIMMO: I'm the best!

MONA: Dad. It's bad. Please?

MIMMO: Please what?

MONA: You know exactly what.

MIMMO: Just imagine that the headache is gone and you'll feel great!

MONA: Imagine the migraine away? Pharmaceutical companies would love that.

MIMMO: You're a writer. If you imagine something hard enough –

MONA: Come on, please?

MIMMO: Mona. No. I told you. I'm not doing that anymore.

MONA: I need your help.

MIMMO: You're going to have to learn to do this on your own.

MONA: No, I need you! What if I wake up tomorrow and it's still there? Beating down my brain until I've lost good writing cells? What if it never goes away? What if this migraine is the one that stays forever or until the tumour in the right side of my head bursts and I die a horrible and excruciating death?

MIMMO: Stick to literature, drama doesn't suit you.

MONA: You'll blame yourself for the rest of your life. Plus, if I have a headache, I'm going to have to go straight back to bed and sleep it off. You'll have to put your groceries away.

MIMMO: I can't do this for you every time.

MONA: You don't have to do it every time. Just this time.

MIMMO: You've said that before.

MONA: But I mean it now.

MIMMO: Fine. But you have to keep your promise.

MONA: This is the last time, I swear.

MIMMO: Not that promise, the other one. Well, this one, too. Both promises.

MONA: Fine. Both promises.

MIMMO: As soon as you come back.

MONA: It's two in the morning. What's the rush?

MIMMO: It's important. It has to be tonight. Swear.

MONA: I said fine.

MIMMO: I want to hear it. The whole thing.

MONA: I will –

MIMMO: I *promise.*

MONA: I promise that I will –

MIMMO: As soon as I come back.

MONA: As soon as I come back, I promise I will learn to make pasta sauce with my dad.

MIMMO: Because why?

MONA: Because I should know how to make it.

MIMMO: And?

MONA: It's shameful that I don't already know.

MIMMO: And… Yes?

MONA: I don't see how it's that shameful, by the way. I don't have a mother. That's a Mom thing, isn't it? Culinary skills?

MIMMO: You had a mother.

MONA: I never met her.

MIMMO: You didn't meet her, no, but it doesn't make you motherless.

MONA: That's exactly what it makes me. I was too difficult to bear, literally.

MIMMO: Culinary skills can be a Dad thing, too, you know.

MONA: Okay. I promise I will be eager and ready to learn at two in the morning for some apparent reason.

MIMMO: And what – you're forgetting one other thing.

MONA: What?

MIMMO: The onions.

MONA: And I will chop all the onions.

MIMMO: Even though you're going to cry when you do it?

MONA: Even though I am going to cry when I do it.

MIMMO: Good. Now, rest your head, my little chipmunk.

She does.

There is a moment in a beautiful song, Mona. If you listen, you'll hear it. Before the grand finale, the crescendo, it's quiet. Nothing seems to be happening. It's the lull. The music builds, slowly, one note after another, and it seems as though there is no purpose to this lull. But you know, people are crazy, you know, because the lull? The lull is the best part. Something is coming. And without the lull, how can you crescendo at all?

MONA closes her eyes. MIMMO begins to hum his theme softly. His voice is tired and faint. As he sings, MONA begins to relax completely. From somewhere in the distance, THE BOY's voice joins MIMMO's. He puts his hand on MONA's temples and pulls the migraine from her head. There is pain in his face as he does this. He blows it into the wind.

THE BOY with the umbrella is running along with the migraine as it floats in the direction of the woman, La Signora STREGA.

La STREGA and MIMMO look at each other for a moment.

MIMMO: You.

STREGA: You.

MIMMO: Here we are. I knew it.

STREGA: Something is coming.

La STREGA disappears. MIMMO is alone for a moment. MONA stirs.

MIMMO: Mona, Mona, you're back, my little chipmunk?

MONA: I'm back. No more headache.

MIMMO: Good.

MONA: Thank you.

MIMMO: You're welcome.

MONA: Was I gone long?

MIMMO: No time at all.

MONA: And now, pasta sauce.

MIMMO: Pasta sauce!

MONA: I promised.

MIMMO: First the onions!

He motions to the table where there is a pile of onions.

MONA: We're starting with the worst part.

MIMMO: Then it'll be over. The only way to build up the resistance is to do it.

MONA: I cry every time. Maybe I'll never build up the resistance.

MIMMO: But you never stop trying. That's the point. I bought fifty onions.

MONA: Trial by fire.

MIMMO: Making sauce, Mona, it's in your blood. Once you learn, you can never unlearn. You're also extremely fortunate because you have the world's best teacher.

MONA: Humility has always been your strength.

MIMMO: Assume your post. Are you ready?

MONA: Um – let me just –

MIMMO: Go!

They start chopping the onions. They both start crying. Despite the tears, they keep chopping. Their tears turn to laughter.

A sudden loud car crash. Blackness. The beating of a heart monitor.

A hospital room. MONA sits watching MIMMO's lifeless body. A moment.

MONA: "To you, your father should be as a god. One that composed your beauties, yea, and one to whom you are but as a form in wax. By him imprinted, and within his power to leave the figure or disfigure it."

She looks to him. Nothing.

10, 9, 8, 7, this is an easy one, Dad, 6, 5, 4, just guess, you know this, 3, 2, 1... *A Midsummer Night's Dream.*

Beat.

You know, orphanhood does wonders for creativity anyway, so you're actually helping me. William Wordsworth was an orphan at twelve. Tolstoy, nine. Shakespeare wasn't an orphan but he was a Taurus and he married Anne Hathaway, who was a pregnant orphan. So that counts in double. Edgar Allen Poe was an orphan at two! Tolkien, John Keats, Edward Albee. All orphans. And all male. So. Thank you for what will likely be a lucrative and famed writing career paving the way for orphans of both genders. I'll just harness my extreme pain and loneliness and write some melancholy piece of genius and everyone will think I'm brilliant forever. Write what I know. Right? Write what I know.

She grabs a napkin and scribbles.

What I know. Dad was in a car accident. Dad is in a coma. Dad is brain-dead. Dad is dying. Dad may as well be dead. See? Brilliant.

She tosses the napkin.

Okay, Dad, you need to come back. Come back. Please come back? We haven't made it through the entire canon yet – I still have to read *Lear* to you. You'll love it – it's all about ungrateful daughters. Please. You haven't won the Shakespeare-quoting game yet! You're getting closer! Dad. I'll be better if you come back, I swear. Way better. I'll hug you publicly, I'll laugh at all your jokes, we'll walk down the streets and people will shake their heads and smile knowingly and say "Like father, like daughter." Because we are a little alike. Right? I may not have your better qualities but I certainly have a lot of your insignificant ones. We both bite our nails in traffic. We eat with our mouths open. We both turn red in the face when our tempers are hot. We are both fully capable of having a real and meaningful dialogue with the television. We pronounce the "b" in "plumber" and it pisses everyone off and that justifies it somehow.

Beat.

I haven't made you proud yet. Remember what you said about just imagine what you want and then you get it? "If you imagine something hard enough…"

She tries to imagine.

I imagine – I imagine – you come back and I become great. I write substantial novels that will change the world and your name is on the front page of every one. And you are really proud of me because I am great and also I make you breakfast on Sunday. Our luck is going to change, Dad – when you wake up. We'll have the best luck. Just come on and open your eyes. I can't do this. I need you.

MIMMO's Theme Song begins. THE BOY runs into the room, barefooted, with his umbrella. He faces MONA for a moment.

A sudden crack of thunder and the rain begins. THE BOY runs off. MONA chases after him.

The Slanted House of La Signora STREGA. STREGA is at the stove. MONA barges in.

Agh!

STREGA: You.

MONA: You. *(Beat.)* Who are you?

STREGA: You just barge into people's homes and ask nosy questions?

MONA: Barge? No – I just ran after the – I followed the, um – well –

STREGA: Get it out.

MONA: You didn't see that little boy with the umbrella?

STREGA: What little boy?

MONA: He had no shoes on? He was – little.

STREGA: Nope.

MONA: Eight years old, tops. Blue umbrella.

STREGA: I didn't see no boy.

MONA: But he was right – he had a charming little face – like – oh God…

STREGA: Like what?

MONA: No one. Nothing.

STREGA: Someone. Something. Who?

MONA: Are you…? Who are you?

STREGA: You smell.

MONA: Sorry?

STREGA: You. Smell.

MONA: I have been outside?

STREGA: I know that smell. It's not outside. Do you always see imaginary boys and break into people's homes, Mona?

MONA: I don't see imaginary boys. There was only one boy. And it was a real boy. Wait – how did you know my – I should go.

A sudden clap of thunder. The front door swings open violently. The rain sweeps in.

Agh! Oh – gross!

STREGA: Move – move!

She towels down the carpet.

MONA: I hate getting wet!

STREGA: What are you afraid of? It's water. Here – dry off!

MONA: I get sick easily.

STREGA: Stop crying! Poor baby child.

MONA: I'm asthmatic, you know.

STREGA: Oh shut up.

MONA: Hypothermia was not on my to-do list for the day!

STREGA: Do you put oregano in your bathwater or something?

MONA: Oregano – the herb?

STREGA: Is there another?

MONA: In my bathwater? No. That's very strange.

STREGA: That's not strange, you're strange.

MONA: Of all the things to bathe in.

STREGA: Why's that strange?

MONA: Of all the herbs, I'd say lavender is far more logical.

STREGA: Is it?

MONA: I don't bathe in oregano. Or any herbs. I have a Bed, Bath, and Beyond collection of bubble bath beads, if you really must know. Oh God, I am soaked!

STREGA: It's definitely oregano. The rain brings the smell out.

MONA: What does that even mean?

STREGA: It's strong on you.

MONA: Maybe you have hypersensitive nostrils.

STREGA: You should sit by the fire. Warm up.

MONA: I don't know that I was planning on sticking around here but thank you –

Another clap of thunder.

STREGA: Sit by the fire. You don't want to get sick now, do you? Sit.

La STREGA moves to the stove.

I'll make tea.

MONA: I don't drink –

STREGA: I think you need some tea.

MONA: Do you have espresso?

STREGA: I have tea.

MONA: Tea?

MIMMO is there, making breakfast.

MIMMO: Tea?

MONA: Yes, tea. Just try it.

MIMMO: We never drink tea. Why would we suddenly start now?

MONA: I don't know; why not?

MIMMO: Because tea is flavoured water and it's disgusting.

MONA: Coffee is also flavoured water.

MIMMO: Espresso isn't water.

MONA: I'm not even going to touch that. Dad, tea is really good for you. Antioxidants and whatever. You drink too much espresso, okay.

MIMMO: Espresso is basically water! And I like it. You drink it too.

MONA: I don't have three pots a day.

MIMMO: Tea is too civilized. We're not civilized people, Mona.

MONA: Ah! Watch, Dad!

MIMMO: What are you "Ah"-ing about?

MONA: Watch your hands! Those eggs are steaming! You have to wait for them to cool off before you peel them.

MIMMO: Am I a child or something? First you lecture me on tea and now, eggs. Let me make the breakfast, okay?

MONA: You're going to burn your hands.

MIMO: I haven't burned them yet.

MONA: Don't complain to me when you've got blisters.

MIMMO: May I remind you that I have been making you breakfast every Sunday since you've been living, and it's always worked out.

MONA: You've been lucky.

MIMMO: I've done it all by myself. Like a big boy. No help from you.

MONA: You will burn your hands one of these days, mark my words, Father o'mine. And I will laugh gleefully at your pain.

MIMMO: How kind of you.

MONA: Stubborn.

MIMMO: Not stubborn. Right. This is how I've been doing it for years.

MONA: You've never burned your hands?

MIMMO: Nope.

MONA: I don't believe you.

MIMMO: You build up a resistance to the heat over time. My mother didn't even use oven gloves.

MONA: But you have to burn yourself a few times before you build up the resistance. You don't just instantly have immunity.

MIMMO: She did. And she taught me when I was a kid. I was making breakfast for her when I was little.

MONA: Subtle.

MIMMO: Eight years old. Peeling eggs for my dear mother.

MONA: You were the greatest kid ever, I'm sure.

MIMMO: I was, yes.

MONA: An eight-year-old chef child.

MIMMO: An eight-year-old genius chef child. Among other things.

MONA: Wow. Must have been hard for you being perfect.

MIMMO: Exhausting.

MONA: How do you live with yourself now?

MIMMO: Now? It's even harder.

MONA: Really?

MIMMO: The coat of greatness only gets thicker with age.

MONA: Saccharine.

MIMMO: Are you bitter? We can't all be child geniuses.

MONA: It would interrupt the order of the world.

MIMMO: We all contribute in our own special ways. You've got your strengths, too.

MONA: I take out the garbage so well.

MIMMO: When you remember, yes. And your dishwashing skills are really improving.

MONA: It's meditation.

MIMMO: You clean the pans without scraping off the Teflon. That's a skill.

MONA: I'm blessed.

MIMMO: Awww, Mona Mona. Poor baby child. Woe, woe is poor Mona. She's skill-less! Nothing to offer! Poor, poor girl – oh SHIT! *(He burns himself.)* Ouch.

He looks at her.

Don't say anything.

MONA: I didn't.

MIMMO: Well don't.

MONA: Are you okay?

MIMMO: I'm fine. It's fine. It's not that bad.

MONA: Okay.

MIMMO: Well anyway the way you eat these eggs is completely wrong. They're better when they're runny.

MONA: I don't like the texture.

MIMMO: You're basically eating rubber.

MONA: Dad.

MIMMO: What?

MONA: Do you want some ice for your hand?

MIMMO: Yes.

She gets the ice and holds it to his hand.

MONA: Poor baby child.

MIMMO: Shush.

MONA: Don't be upset about it. Here, little Mimmo. Since you're handicapped, I, your dutiful daughter, will feed you.

MIMMO: Stop!

MONA: Beautiful Sunday morning eggs from the kitchen of the former genius chef child.

MIMMO: That was the first time that ever happened.

MONA: You build up a resistance to the heat. Eventually you won't feel it. Over time, child, over time.

La STREGA is in MONA's face.

STREGA: Tea!

MONA: Oh – Jesus!

STREGA: What are you looking at it for? You don't stare at it. You drink it.

MONA: It's got chunks.

STREGA: They're herbs. Clearly you're okay with those.

MONA: Isn't tea supposed to be less – thick?

STREGA: Drink it before it gets cold.

MONA: Um – well…

STREGA: Are you afraid of something?

MONA: What – why would you say that?

STREGA: Well, are you?

MONA: Afraid? No.

STREGA: Go ahead then.

MONA: Yeah, I'm going to.

STREGA: Then do it. Drink.

A stare-down. MONA takes a very small sip.

What are you, a bird?

MONA: It's salty.

STREGA: It's flavour.

MONA: What do you put in here?

STREGA: The mashed-up bones of your ancestors.

La STREGA drinks her entire cup of the tea in one gulp.

Herbs. They're just herbs. Don't be such a baby.

MONA: I'm not a baby.

STREGA: Then quit being a chicken and drink your tea. If I was going to kill you, you'd be dead already.

MONA: That's comforting. And I am not a chicken, just to be clear. I am actually really making progress on my impulsivity and reckless living.

STREGA: You seem reckless.

MONA boldly takes another small sip of the tea.

MONA: Great tea! I like salt. Good.

The thunder claps again.

It's raining really hard, isn't it?

STREGA: Yup.

MONA: Wonder when it's going to stop.

STREGA: When it stops.

MONA: Do you ever get nervous when it rains a lot?

STREGA: Why would I get nervous?

MONA: Well. Your house. You know – it's –

STREGA: ...yes?

MONA: Slanted.

STREGA: My house is not slanted.

MONA: The ground beneath it is.

STREGA: That's a very different thing.

MONA: That doesn't make you nervous at all?

STREGA: No.

MONA: But eventually – you know what'll happen, right? *(Beat.)* What are you going to do when the ground beneath you slides away?

STREGA: Slide away with it.

MONA: You are not concerned at all about this very real and obvious hazard?

STREGA: Lived here my whole life. Hasn't happened yet.

MONA: You live here alone?

STREGA: Mm-hm.

MONA: Did your husband die or something?

STREGA: I don't have a husband.

MONA: Oh, right, yeah, that's fine – I didn't mean – you don't have to – I don't have a husband, either. Or a partner or anything.

STREGA: I don't care.

MONA: Nope. None of the above.

STREGA: I'd rather you just drink your tea.

MONA: Well, right, anyway, yeah, but, just saying I don't want one either. A boyfriend.

STREGA: Great.

MONA: Because I'm fine on my own.

STREGA: Tea isn't good when it's cold.

MONA: It's not like I've never dated before. People have been really interested... lots of guys, you know, but I've been in school. Really focused on that. Studying. Well – studied – I'm done now. Graduated. Creative writing. I'm working now. Writing. Like a book. Or something substantial. Still working that out.

STREGA: What's it about?

MONA: What?

STREGA: The substantial book. What's it about?

MONA: Well, I don't know that yet. It takes quite a bit of time.

STREGA: Sounds good.

MONA: I just finished school. Like just.

STREGA: Mm-hm.

MONA: You don't just leap into success after graduation. There is a period of entering the field that is pretty standard.

STREGA: So you're not a writer, then.

MONA: I have a degree in creative writing.

STREGA: But you haven't written anything.

MONA: Well – no, but –

STREGA: So you're not a writer.

MONA: Well…

STREGA: You're not. When you write something, then you'll be a writer. Until then, you're just a talker.

MONA: Thank you.

STREGA: I can't understand why the boys aren't knocking down your door to court you.

MONA: I just said – you know – the boys are knocking on the door – that is not the issue. The door is actually hanging on its hinge because it's been just beat down by the boys. But it doesn't matter because –

STREGA: Because you're fine on your own. Yeah, I see that.

La STREGA refills her own tea cup.

How's the tea?

MONA: Getting tastier with every sip.

STREGA: Great. Then you're ready for more.

La STREGA refills MONA's cup.

MONA: You read my mind.

MONA takes another sip.

STREGA: You must be hungry. I'll make you something.

MONA: There is actually a lot of substance to this tea.

La STREGA chops garlic. Oils a pan.

STREGA: It will only be a few minutes. I work fast.

MONA: Really, I don't need anything.

STREGA: I've already started.

MONA: I should go, anyway.

The thunder again. Loud.

STREGA: I'll make a quick pasta sauce. It's easy. Besides…

MIMMO enters with a bowl of tomatoes.

MIMMO/STREGA: The tomatoes are nice this year.

MONA: I'm not hungry.

MIMMO/STREGA: First you chop the onions!

MIMMO: Even though I cry every time!

MONA: Please, Dad. I'm having a hard time focusing here.

MIMMO: You should learn how to do this yourself, Mona.

MONA: I'm trying to work.

MIMMO: It's shameful that you don't already know.

MONA: I'll learn another time.

MIMMO: Promise?

MONA: Yes. Just please!

MIMMO: All right. I'll hold you to it! Whenever the mood strikes me. You've committed now.

MONA: Dad. Can I please work?

MIMMO: Of course. Sorry.

MIMMO continues cooking while MONA tries to work.

MONA: Ugh. No. Stupid. So stupid.

She writes some more.

That's even worse, Mona!

She is erasing furiously.

MIMMO: Do you think you might take a break? I need help with the salad.

MONA: What is that noise?

MIMMO: I just asked for help with the salad.

MONA: No it's not you. It's faint. Like tiny screaming. What is it?

MIMMO: I don't hear screaming.

MONA: Like *(She tries to demonstrate, then she hears it again.)* That! That sound! There it is. Do you hear that?

MIMMO chuckles.

Is this funny to you? It's very distracting.

MIMMO: It's not screaming.

MONA: I'm having a hard enough time as it is.

MIMMO: It's the garlic, Mona. Humming. Garlic sings when it's in hot olive oil.

MONA: No, it doesn't.

MIMMO: It's like a little orgasm. Garlic orgasms in olive oil.

MONA: Dad. Gross. Don't say org – don't say that.

MIMMO: Orgasm?

MONA: It's really weird.

MIMMO: The only thing that's weird to me is that you can't even say the word.

MONA: I can say the word.

MIMMO: Then say it.

MONA: This is juvenile. I have work to do.

MIMMO: Orgasm.

MONA: Ugh.

He laughs.

MIMMO: It's a funny word, isn't it? Orgasm. Orgasm. You should try saying it. It's fun.

MONA: Oh my God.

MIMMO: Do you say it with your boooooyfriend? With Mikey?? Your loveeeeeeer.

MONA: No. Stop. Right now.

MIMMO: Mikey and Mona sitting in a tree… O R G A S-MIC! First comes –

MONA: Don't talk about him. Just – I don't want to talk about him.

MIMMO: Fine.

MONA: Fine.

MIMMO: How's the novel coming?

MONA: It's a soup of shit.

MIMMO: Shit Soup. Catchy title.

MONA: My professors talk about writing as though it's the most gratifying and painless activity. I can think of four thousand other things that would gratify me more than this.

MIMMO: It'll come to you.

MONA: It never just comes to you.

MIMMO: Use your imagination! You're one of the most imaginative people I know.

MONA: I imagine! I try! And nothing happens. Just an avalanche of –

MIMMO: Shit Soup.

MONA: A novel of epic proportions.

MIMMO: Maybe it's not a novel.

MONA: What?

MIMMO: What if you write something else?

MONA: What else would I write?

MIMMO: Shakespeare.

MONA: You do see the obvious flaw in that suggestion, right?

MIMMO: You've been speaking in verse since you were a kid.

MONA: It's not my verse.

MIMMO: So write your own verse.

MONA: What, a sonnet? Who reads sonnets?

MIMMO: I'm just saying maybe you're not a novelist. Maybe you're a poet.

MONA: No, I'm not a poet.

MIMMO: How do you know?

MONA: Because. Poetry is ephemeral and lazy, frankly. And overly emotional and boring. I'm not that.

MIMMO: Okay.

MONA: Poetry is so bohemian. I might as well play the didgeridoo and shave my head.

MIMMO: Fine.

MONA: And more importantly, who makes a living as a poet? Can you even remember the last time you sat and read a book of poetry? It's a waste of fifteen dollars. The books are eight pages long.

MIMMO: Mona?

MONA: I'm not a poet. I'm not.

MIMMO: Is something else going on here that you're not telling me?

MONA: Writing poetry is like playing the ukulele.

MIMMO: What's wrong, Mona?

MONA: What? Nothing.

MIMMO: Tell me.

MONA: I should work. I have a book of poetry to write.

MIMMO: Where's Mikey tonight? Mona. Where's Mike?

MONA: I don't know.

MIMMO: What happened, honey?

MONA: I don't want to talk about it.

MIMMO: Mona, where is Michael?

MONA: I said I don't know!

MIMMO: Why don't you know?

MONA: Because he broke up with me. That's why.

MIMMO: What?

MONA: He broke up with me.

MIMMO: Broke up? When?

MONA: Today.

MIMMO: Why?

MONA: He's on scholarship, Dad. It's a wonder we've lasted this long.

MIMMO: What does that mean?

MONA: A boy who plays sports doesn't want a serious, committed, awkward, writer girlfriend. He wants girls. With humongous boobs who wear string bikinis and drink Sex on the Beach. I hate sand.

MIMMO: He said he wanted humongous boobs?

MONA: He didn't need to say that.

MIMMO: Break up! What does that mean? You don't break up!

MONA: Maybe *you* don't. It's not part of your ancient love traditions.

MIMMO: My ancient love traditions are not ancient, they're effective.

MONA: Don't lecture me now, Dad.

MIMMO: You know, it's a verb, you know! You love. You choose. You commit. You work. You don't BREAK UP!

MONA: Some people do.

MIMMO: How dare he? I opened myself to him. I let him in my home, cooked for him, how many meals? Good meals, too. Remember those lamb skewers I made?

MONA: I don't think it was the lamb.

MIMMO: I marinated that lamb for four days!

MONA: He loved the lamb.

MIMMO: And now he just BREAKS UP like it meant nothing?

MONA: Yes, he does.

MIMMO: That is a boy, that's what that is! A BOY – not a MAN! He didn't even discuss this with me! We could have worked something out! We had such good communication, the two of us.

MONA: What is there to discuss?

MIMMO: What's wrong with him? How could he do this to me? I treated him like a son!

MONA: He doesn't want me, Dad.

MIMMO: He wasn't right for us anyway.

MONA: Listen to yourself. ME. He left ME. You actually have nothing to do with this.

MIMMO: He was a part of this family.

MONA: He loves you. His biggest concern when he dumped me was whether or not you'd lose respect for him.

MIMMO: It was – really?

MONA: He probably would have left long ago if not for your marinated lamb skewers and dude love.

MIMMO: Don't say that.

MONA: Say what? I may be your kid but if you can fathom this, I don't share your brilliant charm.

MIMMO: Honey.

MONA: I'm moody, inconsiderate, selfish, fucking pretentious. I talk talk talk such stupidity. I'm boring and awkward and nervous.

MIMMO: You're not awkward.

MONA: Mike is social and innately likeable. We would go to parties and he would actually converse with people! And enjoy it! Sound familiar?

MIMMO: Stop.

MONA: He's just like you. He's GREAT. A great guy who has endless charm.

MIMMO: Mona, you are very –

MONA: Don't waste your time, Dad! You might as well face it now. I'm not you. I'm not going to blossom into this perfect mirror image of all your best qualities. I'm not your fucking masterpiece. I'm a mess!

La STREGA holds a plate out to MONA.

MIMMO/STREGA: Pasta is ready.

MONA: I don't feel very well.

STREGA: Probably just the rain. Gets into your bones. Have something to eat. It'll make you stronger.

MONA: I don't want anything to eat. Ugh.

STREGA: Migraine?

MONA: What?

STREGA: Is it your head?

MONA: How did you – No. It's not my head. I should go.

MONA goes to the door. The thunder crashes and wind blows.

STREGA: "Wind, rain, and thunder, remember Earthly Man is but a Substance that must yield to you."

MONA: *Pericles.*

STREGA: You know Shakespeare?

MONA: I have to go.

STREGA: Not quite yet, Mona.

MONA tries opening the door. The thunder claps and the rain gushes in.

"Blow winds and crack your cheeks! Rage! Blow! Rumble thy bellyful! Spit, fire! Spout, rain! Smite flat the thick rotundity o'th'world, crack nature's molds, all germens spill at once that make ungrateful man!"

MONA: Who are you?

STREGA: Just rest your head, little chipmunk.

MONA: How…?

STREGA: You're not the only person I know who smells of oregano. Another friend of mine carries around that same scent. You know him. He calls you "chipmunk." For your big teeth and your little face, which annoys you because you hate your teeth. You don't smile that often because of them. He annoys you a lot, actually, though you'd rather not admit it. Then everyone would know what a pernicious daughter you are. But the reality is his incessant optimism, his hopefulness, both of which you did not inherit, disgust you. Embarrass you. But mostly, they terrify you. Because now, he is in a hospital bed, listening to the music of the heart monitor keeping him alive, his brain one big pile of mush. Strange, isn't it? One minute he's teaching you to make pasta sauce at two in the morning, and the next, he's falling asleep at the wheel while driving to work in a clearly unreliable piece of metal. His car flipping over over over over until it throws him up onto the street. What are you going to do, little chipmunk? Now that he won't be there to blow your migraines into the air, to sing your nerves to sleep? What incredibly inconvenient timing. Right in the middle of your post-graduate bubble.

THE BOY runs through the space humming Mimmo's Theme.

I met our mutual friend a long, long time ago. Mimmo Con La Voce he was called then. I came to him and I stayed with him. When he was only a little boy. Running barefoot under his blue umbrella. Oregano wafting through the streets as he ran by. Humming a familiar melody. And now, I come to you.

MONA: I know who you are.

STREGA: I come in shape rounder than a bulbous nose in a chariot of ripe, purple fig. With my team of garlic cloves and oregano leaves, I come to young dreamers. This is I. Once I come, I never leave.

MONA: This is… she.

STREGA: And in this state –

MONA: She gallops night by night through dreamers' brains –

STREGA: And then they dream of –

MONA: The past.

STREGA: To dream of the past is to face the future.

MONA: La Strega.

STREGA: You don't feel so great, do you? A little tired, perhaps, weak. Don't be nervous. You drank a tea that I brew – it will drain the pain from your hipbones where we carry our greatest fears. You're going on a little trip, Mona, a trip back. There are things you should see. But seeing clearly can't happen until you are in the deepest and soundest of…

MONA falls into a deep sleep. La STREGA catches her.

Sleep.

A flourish. We are back in time. THE BOY, MIMMO Con La Voce, rushes into La STREGA's home as MONA did.

MIMMO: Agh!

STREGA: Agh!

MIMMO: You!

STREGA: You!

MIMMO: Who are you?

STREGA: You just barge into people's homes asking nosy questions?

MIMMO: Barge? I didn't barge.

STREGA: You didn't knock.

MIMMO: You should really try locking the front door if you don't want anyone to come in.

Sounds from outside. Boys screaming, stones being thrown.

STREGA: What is that?

MIMMO: My friends.

STREGA: Friends? You run away from your friends?

MIMMO: Well, not my friends at all, really.

STREGA: I should think not.

MIMMO: They're horrible.

STREGA: My windows will shatter from their rocks if you don't hurry out of here.

MIMMO: Oh, I can't! They'll beat me if I go outside.

STREGA: Well, beat them back.

MIMMO: Can't I stay for a few minutes? For coffee?

STREGA: Coffee?

MIMMO: Espresso.

STREGA: You're a child!

MIMMO: I take twelve sugars. Do you have cookies?

STREGA: How old are you?

MIMMO: Eight.

STREGA: You're a little articulate for eight, wouldn't you say?

MIMMO: Oh, I'm a genius child.

STREGA: Where are your shoes?

MIMMO: You must have cookies in here. How can you have espresso without cookies?

STREGA: Stay out of my kitchen. There is no espresso in this house.

MIMMO: No espresso?

STREGA: No coffee. Only tea.

MIMMO: Tea?

STREGA: Tea.

MIMMO: Oh! I know who you are! I have heard stories about you!

STREGA: Have you.

MIMMO: You're La Strega. That's what they call you!

STREGA: They?

MIMMO: Even my mom told me about you! All the people of the piazza know you, Strega! I know all the stories.

STREGA: I'm sure they're gripping.

MIMMO: "The unmarried woman will become La Strega on the eve of her third decade." Her lady tubes burst open and she instantly grows a beard and develops a limp to compensate for the large mass of skin that grows on her shoulder. It rains in the piazza for thirty days after that and all the children of the town scream in their sleep to mourn for the babies that she will never have.

STREGA: A pretty picture.

MIMMO: But you're special. And so is the tea you brew. Your house on the slanted hill can slide away and disappear in an instant! I heard a story about your mother, too!

STREGA: Enough.

MIMMO: Are you really La Strega?

STREGA: What do you think?

MIMMO: You look like a normal woman to me. Pretty, even.

STREGA: How kind.

MIMMO: I'm not afraid of you.

STREGA: You're not?

MIMMO: You're not even scary or anything.

STREGA: You should be afraid, Mimmo Con La Voce.

MIMMO: How do you know my name?

STREGA: I've heard stories, too. I know more than just your name.

MIMMO: You are La Signora Strega! I knew it!

STREGA: And you are Mimmo Con La Voce. The Little Boy with the Voice. That's what they call you.

MIMMO: We both have nicknames!

STREGA: The boy who carries the scent of oregano wherever he goes. The piazza is small, so I know exactly where you are at all times, Mimmo. My nose is tuned in to the smell of herbs, you know. I can smell you as you run through the piazza. Humming your song. All the men's heads drooping slowly as you skip by, their cigarettes dangling from their mouths and their playing cards blowing away in the wind. You came from your mother's belly singing with that voice of yours. It was the easiest birth in the history of all births. I know all about what that voice of yours can do, Mimmo. You sing your song, melancholy and sweet, and your music relaxes your victims so deeply that the fears that live in the marrow of their bones slide away into the wind.

MIMMO: Wow.

STREGA: I don't believe in stories. Those "friends" of yours still throw stones and most of the time you're running, it's away.

MIMMO: We're the same kind.

STREGA: You and me?

MIMMO: I'm not a witch but we're the same kind.

STREGA: I told you. I don't believe those stories I hear.

MIMMO: You've heard the stories, but have you heard the voice?

STREGA: Don't you dare.

MIMMO sings his theme song. His voice is light and sweet. He does nothing physically, only sends his voice to La STREGA, who is lulled into a state of deep relaxation, not quite asleep. She is quiet.

MIMMO puts his hands on La STREGA's forehead and pulls her sadness from her, much like he did with MONA's head earlier.

A moment. The stones and the calls can still be heard.

It's not easy being one of our kind. Always running away. Always alone. There is a lot to fear, little Mimmo. Believe me. And we can't always hide here in the kitchen where it's warm.

A flourish. We are in another moment from the past. Years later.

Aha! I win! *(She laughs.)*

MIMMO: Again?

STREGA: Again! Again!

MIMMO: But how? I don't see how you won that time!

STREGA: You don't see! That's your problem! Open your eyes.

MIMMO: I see just fine! You're cheating.

STREGA: No, I am not!

She lays out all of the cards in front of him and closes her eyes.

Go on, pick a card. Even with my eyes closed, I see better than you do.

A moment. MIMMO reaches for a card swiftly. She beats him to it.

MIMMO: Hey! How did you do that?

He reaches again. She beats him.

You know which card I'm going to choose! You must be cheating.

STREGA: I don't read minds. I make tea.

MIMMO: It's not fair. Cheater.

STREGA: No cheating. Just listening.

MIMMO: You listen with your ears, not your eyes.

STREGA: Maybe you do. But true listening is with the whole body.

MIMMO: Play again!

STREGA: I'm done playing for now.

MIMMO: No. Again.

STREGA: Another time.

MIMMO: I want to win.

STREGA: You can't win every time.

MIMMO: Let's play again.

STREGA: No.

MIMMO: I'm tired of losing. I HAVE TO WIN.

STREGA: Today, you lose.

MIMMO: No NO NO. I'm not leaving until I win.

STREGA: Stubborn, Mimmo. You can't win like that.

MIMMO: One more game.

STREGA: No more games. Sit in your loss.

MIMMO: Come ON. We'll switch.

STREGA: Switch?

MIMMO: You reach for the card and I'll guess which one you pick.

STREGA: You're confident.

MIMMO: I know I can win.

STREGA: How do you know?

MIMMO: I'm Mimmo Con La Voce. I can do anything.

She laughs. A moment.

STREGA: Both eyes closed?

MIMMO: That's right.

He lays out the cards and closes his eyes. A moment. She reaches for a card. He lunges. He is way off. He opens his eyes.

STREGA: You lose.

MIMMO: NO!

He takes his hand and waves it across the table, sending all the cards flying.

Another flourish, another moment in time. Years later.

Signora! Signora, wake up!

STREGA: Mimmo? Do you know what time it is?

MIMMO: It's important. Life or death! Do you have espresso on?

STREGA: How many times must we go through this?

MIMMO: Oh, I won't sleep for days, espresso or no!

STREGA: Are you crazy?

MIMMO: Yes, I am!

STREGA: Don't you have school soon? It's early morning.

MIMMO: Signora, at times like these, school, books, teachers, who needs them? Today, the world is so much bigger than it's ever been before! It's huge.

STREGA: It's puberty.

MIMMO: Love, Signora, love! I'm in real true lasting love!

STREGA: Nothing lasts.

MIMMO: This will.

STREGA: Oh, Mimmo, ever the hopeful.

MIMMO: Teresa! The most beautiful name! The most beautiful face!

STREGA: Domenico Zappa's daughter, Teresa? The one who lives by the marina?

MIMMO: She's the most beautiful thing I've ever seen! Shy and sweet! She could barely look at my eyes all night without turning pink! It means she loves me, too.

STREGA: Maybe it means she was warm.

MIMMO: No! She was shivering! It was freezing by the water tonight.

STREGA: Well, did you give her a coat?

MIMMO: I didn't have one.

STREGA: Oh my God.

MIMMO: Is that bad?

STREGA: Really bad. It's common courting etiquette.

MIMMO: But I didn't have a coat.

STREGA: You just let her shiver? That cold probably went straight to her heart and froze any warm feelings she had toward you.

MIMMO: Oh no! I have to go back and apologize!

STREGA: Domenico Zappa has the biggest temper in the town! Don't go poking around his house at this hour unless you want to end up dead.

MIMMO: I'm going to ask him for her hand.

STREGA: In marriage?

MIMMO: Tomorrow morning.

STREGA: You spend one night walking along the marina and you want to get married?

MIMMO: Yes!

STREGA: You're still a boy, Mimmo. Sixteen is too young!

MIMMO: No, it's not.

STREGA: You're not thinking. Something like this requires thought, deliberation.

MIMMO: Sometimes thinking too much can ruin things, Signora. Sometimes you just have to jump.

STREGA: But at the end of the jump, you will always fall.

MIMMO: Congratulate me, Signora, I'm getting MARRIED! Be happy, for once!

STREGA: Too fast, Mimmo; stop and take a breath!

MIMMO: Okay, fine!

He stops, breathes in, and lets out a gleeful scream.

I'll go home and have a cold shower – good for circulation. I'll put on my best shirt, the blue one or maybe the green one? The blue one. Then I'll walk straight to her house and introduce her father to his son-in-law!

STREGA: Stop! Look, you may feel…

MIMMO: Tingly?

STREGA: Whatever. You may feel that now, but those feelings go away. They don't last forever. Nothing lasts forever. Stop and think first. Consider all the possibilities, and there are many. It may not end the way you imagine right now.

MIMMO: If I imagine hard enough, it can be exactly the way I want it to. Exactly.

A flourish. We are in another moment in the past. MIMMO sits with wrapped baby MONA in his arms. He is dishevelled. The baby is crying. La STREGA sits near him or stands in a doorway. He tries to quiet the baby down. He tries to hum to her, but his voice cracks. A moment. He speaks into the sky.

Teresa, you need to come back. Come back. Please come back? Please. She needs you! I need you! I'll be better if you come back, I swear. Way better. I'll relax more. Deal with my moodiness! Calm my temper. I won't have to be right all the time! Please, Teresa. I don't know what to do. I'm lost.

I haven't done anything great yet.

I imagine – I imagine – you come back and I become great. I change the world and we raise our family and you are really proud of me because I am great. Our luck is going change, Teresa. We'll have the best luck. Just come back. I can't do this. I need you.

The baby cries more loudly. She is inconsolable.

I am Mimmo Con La Voce and I can do anything. I can do anything.

MIMMO starts to sing to the baby MONA. His voice is tired and strained. Her cries just get louder.

MIMMO breaks down. He stops singing. La STREGA reaches for him. He turns away from her. She fades away in darkness.

He is alone with the baby. A moment.

Baby MONA's cry suddenly changes into a single note. A moment. MIMMO looks to the baby MONA, astonished and torn. The baby is singing to him. Her song relaxes MIMMO.

A flourish. Back in La STREGA's kitchen, the present. MONA wakes.

STREGA: Do you know what my mother was called? Gialla Maria, for her eyes. She had these piercing yellow eyes. She was crazy. A witch. My father was a general coming to give a speech in our town. He saw my mother in the crowd, standing alone, of course, and those yellow eyes transfixed him, buried themselves deep into his chest. He stopped his speech midway through it, left the stage, and followed the sway of my mother's hips straight to her bed. The people of the piazza still tell the stories of the moans they heard coming from her house on that night. When she woke up in the morning, the general was lying dead in her bed. The ecstasy of love killed him. I was born nine months later. And my life was just me and my mother. She died when I was twelve. The ones that burn the brightest – those are the fires that go out first.

MONA: That baby that my dad was holding. The baby that was singing.

STREGA: You.

MONA: Me.

STREGA: Turns out you have a fire of your own.

The rain stops. We hear the water flowing down the slanted hill toward the river.

MONA: He never told me.

STREGA: It's a lonely life being one of our kind. Mimmo knew that.

MONA: Is he going to go away?

STREGA: I'm an old woman now. Old. And do you know what I see every night before I go to sleep and every morning when I wake up?

MONA: What?

STREGA: My mother's yellow eyes. Some things never go away.

THE BOY appears, the blue umbrella in his hand.

Death happens, Mona. We can do nothing to stop that. Not even our kind. The story rarely works out the way we want it to. But sometimes…

THE BOY starts to sing.

It can be exactly as you imagine.

THE BOY runs. MONA turns after him. The heart monitor sounds.

We are back in the hospital room. MIMMO's body is still in the same place. The closed blue umbrella now lies on the edge of the hospital bed.

MONA: Sometimes, it can be exactly as I imagine.

Beat. She turns away from the hospital bed.

I imagine – This is not how you go, Dad. No! No beeping monitors, no pulling plugs, no wooden caskets or cheese platters or obituaries or condolences. No death! There is no death.

MONA closes her eyes. A moment.

There is only the sun shining and the river glistening. Warm and quiet and flowing and ready. And there's you and there's me. You're dressed in your suit with the bowtie and the handkerchief. And they don't match. And you've got that torn brown leather suitcase with you. And you're not biting your nails because you're just going on a trip. And we're not sad because we know. We know that you never actually go away. A part of you stays. So we don't cry. Instead, we sing.

MIMMO's eyes flutter open slowly.

And you sail away, Mimmo Con La Voce. My dad. You just sail away. On a bed of oregano while the sun lights you on your way.

Mimmo's Theme plays. MIMMO stands. He takes the bandage from his head and puts on the bowtie and handkerchief. He picks up his suitcase.

He races out of the hospital room. MONA grabs the umbrella and runs after him.

The river. The bed of oregano waits. MONA catches up to MIMMO. They face the river.

Handsome.

MIMMO: The old man's still got it.

MONA: I knew you'd hate that hospital. You're lucky you were eating through a tube. The food is gross.

MIMMO: Who eats Jello?

MONA: It's pigskin, you know.

MIMMO: Ew.

MONA: "Thou know'st 'tis common all that lives must die passing through nature to eternity." 10, 9, 8…

MIMMO: *Hamlet.*

MONA: *Hamlet.*

MIMMO: Yes! Got it!

MONA: We're going on different trips now, huh, Dad.

MIMMO: Yes.

MONA: I'm scared.

MIMMO: I know.

MONA: Are you scared? It's okay if you are.

MIMMO: A little. Not really. Yes. I'm scared.

MONA: There is a moment in a beautiful song. If you listen, you'll hear it. Before the grand finale, the crescendo, it's quiet. Nothing seems to be happening.

MIMMO: It's the lull.

MONA: The music builds, slowly, one note after another. It seems as though there is no purpose to this lull. But you know, people are crazy, you know, because the lull?

MIMMO: The lull is the best part.

MONA: Something is coming.

MIMMO: Something great.

MONA: And without the lull?

MIMMO: How can you crescendo at all?

He puts his hand to his chest and grabs his voice. He gives it to MONA. A grand and simple gesture.

I'll be in there.

MONA: Once I learn, I can't unlearn.

MIMMO: Not when you've had the best teacher.

MONA: The very best.

MIMMO: I would know. I've had you.

MONA: Bye, Dad.

MIMMO: Bye.

MIMMO takes the umbrella and holds his suitcase on his bed of oregano. MONA starts to sing; MIMMO joins her and floats away, smiling. The sun is shining. MONA finishes the song alone.

A moment as MONA takes in the audience.

MONA: A Sonnet.

In my imagination my dad stands,
A light so bright that shames the twinkling stars,
And in the palms of his working hands,
My heart will lie for all eternities to come.
I look above as he does below,
The pulsing blood we share runs through my veins,
And in it strength to face what's yet to come,
With boldness that he has heaven ordained.
And who can say to where our bodies go?
When breath has breathed its last, time takes its claim?
But in the corners only kings can dwell,
The boy will sing and laugh away his days.
    And here today, this girl shall face her fate,
    So brave on earth, for she is finally great.

Lights fade to black.

The End.